quick & easy

asri sahari

Marshall Cavendish
Cuisine

Designer: Steven Tan
Series Designer: Bernard Go Kwang Meng

Copyright © 2011 Marshall Cavendish International (Asia) Private Limited

Published by Marshall Cavendish Cuisine
An imprint of Marshall Cavendish International
1 New Industrial Road, Singapore 536196

Other Marshall Cavendish Offices:
Marshall Cavendish International. PO Box 65829 London EC1P 1NY, UK • Marshall Cavendish Corporation. 99 White Plains Road, Tarrytown NY 10591-9001, USA • Marshall Cavendish International (Thailand) Co Ltd. 253 Asoke, 12th Flr, Sukhumvit 21 Road, Klongtoey Nua, Wattana, Bangkok 10110, Thailand • Marshall Cavendish (Malaysia) Sdn Bhd, Times Subang, Lot 46, Subang Hi-Tech Industrial Park, Batu Tiga, 40000 Shah Alam, Selangor Darul Ehsan, Malaysia

Marshall Cavendish is a trademark of Times Publishing Limited

National Library Board Singapore Cataloguing in Publication Data

Asri Sahari, 1974-
Quick & easy / Asri Sahari. – Singapore : Marshall Cavendish Cuisine, c2011.
p. cm. – (Mini cookbooks)
ISBN : 978-981-4351-51-5

1. Quick and easy cooking. I. Title. II. Series: Mini cookbooks.

TX833.5
641.555 -- dc22   OCN728078647

Printed in Singapore by KWF Printing Pte Ltd

contents

portobello mushrooms with hazelnut gremolata Serves 2

INGREDIENTS

Portobello mushrooms	4, medium, stems removed
Olive oil	1 Tbsp
Salt and pepper	to taste
Chevril	1 sprig
Sage	1 sprig

GREMOLATA

Hazelnuts	500 g (1 lb 1 1/2 oz), coarsely chopped
Garlic	2 cloves, peeled and finely chopped
Parsley	55 g (2 oz) , finely chopped
Lemon zest	2 Tbsp, finely chopped
Salt and pepper	to taste

METHOD

- Brush mushrooms on both sides with olive oil and season with salt and pepper. Grill for 5 minutes until cooked.

- To prepare gremolata, combine all the ingredients in a bowl and season with salt and pepper to taste.

- Sprinkle gremolata on top of mushrooms and garnish with chevril and sage before serving.

Front: Prawns in Spicy Garlic Sauce
Back: Portobello Mushrooms with Hazelnut Gremolata

prawns in spicy garlic sauce Serves 2

INGREDIENTS

Prawns (shrimps)	280 g (10 oz), peeled and deveined
Olive oil	1 Tbsp
Garlic	3 cloves, peeled and finely chopped
Dried chillies	3, seeded and crushed
Paprika	$1/3$ tsp
Parsley	1 Tbsp, finely chopped
Coriander leaves (cilantro)	1 sprig

METHOD

• Rinse prawns and pat dry. Llightly grease an ovenproof casserole with olive oil and arrange prawns in casserole in a single layer.

• Sprinkle garlic, dried chillies and paprika.

• Bake for 5 minutes in a pre-heated oven at 230°C (450°F) or until prawns are cooked.

• Remove from the oven and sprinkle parsley over.

• Arrange on serving dish, garnish with parsley and coriander leaves and serve hot.

Photograph on page 9

wild mushroom soup Serves 2

INGREDIENTS

Butter	30 g (1 oz)
Shallot	1, peeled and chopped
Shiitake mushrooms	70 g (2½ oz), chopped
Portobello mushrooms	50 g (2 oz), chopped
Chicken stock	500 ml (16 fl oz / 2 cups)
Double (heavy) cream	125 ml (4 fl oz / ½ cup)
Salt and pepper	to taste
Chinese chives	1 sprig

N O T E

To make chicken stock, place a 1.5 kg (3 lb 4½ oz) whole chicken, 2 onions and 1 celery in a large pot and cover with 1.5 litres (48 fl oz / 6 cups) water. Bring to the boil and skim off any surface scum before seasoning with salt and pepper to taste. Simmer for 2 hours while skimming continuously. Strain before using. Otherwise, you can use ready-made chicken stock available from supermarkets.

METHOD

- Melt butter in a pan over medium heat. Sauté shallots and mushrooms for about 5 minutes or until soft.

- Stir in chicken stock and cook for 5 minutes or until thick and bubbly.

- Stir in the cream and season with salt and pepper. Allow to simmer but not boil.

- Ladle soup into a serving bowl and garnish with Chinese chives. Serve hot.

Photograph on page 10

Front: Warm Red Cabbage Salad
Back: Wild Mushroom Soup

warm red cabbage salad Serves 2

INGREDIENTS

Walnuts	125 g (4½ oz), halved
Olive oil	2½ Tbsp
Onion	1, peeled and thinly sliced
Garlic	1 clove, peeled and finely chopped
Red chilli	1, seeded and chopped
Balsamic vinegar	2½ Tbsp
Red cabbage	1 small head, finely shredded
Salt and pepper	to taste
Parsley	1 Tbsp, finely chopped
Marjoram	½ tsp, finely chopped
Chinese chives	1 sprig

METHOD

• Preheat oven to 180°C (350°F).

• Toss walnuts in 1 Tbsp olive oil and season to taste.

• Spread walnuts on a baking tray and toast for 5–7 minutes until fragrant. Remove from oven and let it cool.

• Heat olive oil in a pan over medium heat. Sauté onion, garlic and chilli for 30 seconds.

• Stir in vinegar and cook for 30 seconds more.

• Add cabbage while stirring for about 3 minutes. Season well with salt and pepper.

• Carefully stir in parsley, marjoram and walnuts. Toss together briefly and remove from heat.

• Arrange salad on a serving dish, garnish with Chinese chives and serve warm.

asparagus and red capsicum salad Serves 2

INGREDIENTS

Red capsicums (bell peppers)	2, cored and cut in half
Asparagus	900 g (2 lb), cleaned and trimmed
Onion	1, peeled and thinly sliced
Cos lettuce	100 g (3½ oz), mixed red and green varieties
Basil leaves	1 sprig

DRESSING

Lemon juice	2 Tbsp
Extra virgin olive oil	6 Tbsp
Salt and pepper	to taste

METHOD

- Preheat the grill to 230°C (450°F).

- Place capsicums on a roasting tray and grill for 7–10 minutes. Turn over when it starts to blacken.

- Transfer grilled capsicums to a bowl and cover with plastic wrap. Leave for a few minutes until skin starts to loosen. Skin and thinly slice capsicums. Place into a mixing bowl.

- Slice asparagus and steam for 3 minutes or until tender. Add to mixing bowl.

- Whisk dressing ingredients in a bowl until smooth and pour over vegetables. Toss salad with dressing.

- Line serving bowl with cos lettuce and arrange salad on top. Garnish with basil leaves and serve immediately.

tomato basil soup Serves 2

INGREDIENTS

Olive oil	1 Tbsp
Onion	55 g (2 oz), peeled and diced
Tomatoes	2, diced
Basil leaves	15 g (½ oz) + more for garnishing
Chicken stock (page 9)	250 ml (8 fl oz / 1 cup)
Double (heavy) cream	125 ml (4 fl oz / ½ cup)
Tomato juice	250 ml (8 fl oz / 1 cup)
Salt and pepper	to taste

METHOD

- Heat oil in a pot over medium heat. Stir in onion and cook until soft. Add tomatoes, basil leaves and chicken stock.

- Reduce heat to low and simmer soup for 15 minutes. Set soup aside to cool slightly.

- Purée soup in a food processor. Do this in batches if necessary. Return soup to the pot and simmer over low heat. Stir in cream and season with salt and pepper.

- Ladle into serving bowls and garnish with basil. Serve hot.

classic french onion soup Serves 2

INGREDIENTS

Beef stock	1 litre (32 fl oz / 4 cups)
Onions	3, large, peeled and finely chopped
Sugar	1 tsp
Salt and pepper	to taste
Bread	6 slices, cut into cubes
Edam cheese	125 g (4½ oz), grated
Parsley	1 sprig

METHOD

- Heat 180 ml (6 fl oz / ¾ cup) beef stock in a pot and cook onions for 30 minutes, stirring frequently.

- Add the rest of the stock and sugar. Season with salt and pepper and boil for another 30 minutes.

- While soup is cooking, arrange bread cubes on a baking tray and sprinkle cheese over. Place in a preheated oven at 180°C (350°F) and toast for about 5 minutes or until brown.

- Ladle soup in serving bowls and top with croutons. Garnish with parsley. Serve hot.

Front: Asparagus with Hollandaise Sauce
Back: Classic French Onion Soup

asparagus with hollandaise sauce Serves 2

INGREDIENTS

Asparagus	20 spears, trimmed and blanched
Red capsicum (bell pepper)	1/4, finely chopped
Portabello Button mushrooms	2, cleaned and stem removed
Chevril	1 sprig

SAUCE

Water	4 Tbsp
Lemon juice	2 Tbsp
Bay leaf	1
Spring onions (scallions)	2, finely chopped
Black peppercorns	1 tsp
Egg yolks	3
Butter	185 g (6½ oz), cut into cubes

METHOD

- Prepare sauce. Combine water, lemon juice, bay leaf, spring onions and peppercorns in a pan.

- Bring mixture to a boil, then reduce heat and simmer until liquid is reduced to 2 Tbsp. Strain and reserve liquid. Leave aside to cool.

- When sauce is cool, add egg yolks and place in a bain-marie over simmering water. Whisk mixture until thick.

- Whisk in a few cubes of butter at a time until well mixed. Whisk for 10 minutes or until mixture thickens.

- Hollow out portabello mushroom and spoon sauce over. Garnish with chevril and arrange on serving dish.

- Arrange asparagus beside mushroom on a serving dish, drizzle some sauce on top and sprinkle capsicum over. Serve warm.

Photograph on page 17

beef with caramelised onions Serves 2

INGREDIENTS

Ground paprika	¼ Tbsp
Freshly ground black pepper	¼ tsp
Olive oil	½ Tbsp
Rib-eye steaks	2 kg (4 lb 6 oz), deboned and cut into 2-cm (1-in) slices
Salt	to taste
Chevril	1 sprig

CARAMELISED ONIONS

Beef stock (page 16)	125 ml (4 fl oz / ½ cup)
Sugar	125 g (4½ oz)
Onions	2, peeled and thinly sliced
Red wine vinegar	100 ml (3⅓ fl oz)

METHOD

- Mix paprika, black pepper and olive oil in a small bowl and blend to form a paste. Rub mixture over steaks.

- Place steaks in a baking pan, cover and refrigerate for 3 hours.

- Prepare caramelised onions. Heat beef stock and half the sugar over medium heat. Add onions and red wine vinegar and cook until onions are soft. Strain off liquid and discard.

- Dissolve remaining sugar and reduce heat to low. Cook for another 30–40 minutes or until mixture thickens. Set aside.

- Remove steaks from refrigerator and sprinkle salt over steaks.

- Heat a non-stick frying pan and fry steak to desired doneness. For medium-rare steaks, pan-fry for 5 minutes on each side.

- Arrange steaks on serving dish and top with caramelised onions and mashed potatoes (see page 21). Garnish with chevril and serve hot.

Photograph on page 20

mashed potatoes Serves 2

INGREDIENTS

Potatoes	2, peeled and quartered
Butter	15 g (½ oz)
Milk	2 tsp
Salt and pepper	to taste

METHOD

- Boil potatoes in salted water for 5 minutes and simmer for another 10 minutes.

- Transfer potatoes to a large mixing bowl.

- Add butter and milk, and mash potatoes. Whip mashed potatoes for 1–2 minutes with an electric mixer on medium speed.

- Season with salt and pepper to taste.

smoked salmon and watercress salad Serves 2

INGREDIENTS

Sashimi-grade fresh salmon	450 g (1 lb), cubed
Olive oil	1 Tbsp
Smoked salmon	100 g (3½ oz), thinly sliced
Coriander leaves (cilantro)	1 sprig, chopped
Salt and pepper	to taste
Balsamic vinegar	1 tsp
Extra virgin olive oil	180 ml (6 fl oz / ¾ cup)
Watercress	100 g (3½ oz), shredded
Cherry tomato	1, quartered

METHOD

• Drizzle fresh salmon with olive oil.

• Add smoked salmon, coriander, salt and pepper. Place in wax paper and set aside for 30 minutes.

• Mix vinegar and extra virgin olive oil in a bowl.

• Arrange watercress on 2 serving dishes and arrange salmon around it. Garnish with cherry tomato.

• Drizzle dressing over the salad and serve immediately.

pan-fried red snapper with coriander salsa
Serves 2

INGREDIENTS

Tomatoes	2, peeled, seeded and finely chopped
White wine vinegar (optional)	2 Tbsp
Extra virgin olive oil	2 Tbsp
Red snapper	300 g (10½ oz), cleaned and rinsed
Olive oil	2 Tbsp
Coriander leaves (cilantro)	1 sprig, shredded

CORIANDER SALSA

Garlic	2 cloves, peeled and crushed
Coriander leaves (cilantro)	15 g (½ oz)
Grated lemon zest	1 Tbsp
Lemon juice	2 Tbsp
Cumin powder	2 tsp
Tomato paste	2 Tbsp
Sugar	1 Tbsp
Extra virgin olive oil	85 ml (2½ fl oz / ⅓ cup)

METHOD

- Combine ingredients for salsa, except olive oil, in a blender. Blend until fine, adding extra virgin olive oil gradually.

- Mix tomatoes, vinegar and extra virgin olive oil in a bowl and set mixture aside.

- Cut 3–4 slashes across both sides of the fish and brush with half the coriander salsa.

- Heat olive oil in a pan and pan-fry fish until browned on both sides. Brush remaining salsa on the fish while cooking.

- Dish out onto serving plates and drizzle tomato mixture over fish. Garnish with coriander leaves and serve hot.

Front: Pan-fried Red Snapper with Coriander Salsa
Back: Prawn Tabouleh

prawn tabouleh Serves 2

INGREDIENTS

Bulgur wheat	85 g (3 oz)
Warm water	250 ml (8 fl oz / 1 cup)
Lemon juice	from 3 lemons
Garlic	2 cloves, peeled and crushed
Salt and pepper	to taste
Mint	30 g (1 oz), chopped
Parsley	125 g (4½ oz), chopped
Spring onions (scallions)	30 g (1 oz), finely sliced
Tomatoes	3, diced
Medium prawns (shrimps)	8, peeled, deveined and blanched
Extra virgin olive oil	1–4 Tbsp

NOTE

Extra virgin olive oil and olive oil are used in different ways in Mediterranean cooking. Extra virgin olive oil is usually used for frying or stir-frying while olive oil, which has a higher smoke point, is usually used for deep-frying.

METHOD

• Cover bulgur wheat with warm water and leave to soak for 15 minutes. Drain excess water.

• Mix in lemon juice, garlic, salt and pepper. Set aside for 30 minutes or until bulgur mixture is soft.

• Add mint, parsley, spring onions, tomatoes to bulgur mixture.

• Add prawns and toss with olive oil as desired. Add salt and pepper to taste.

• Place in a serving bowl and serve.

Photograph on page 25

sautéed garlic mushrooms Serves 2

INGREDIENTS

Olive oil	100 ml (3$\frac{1}{3}$ fl oz)
Button mushrooms	450 g (1 lb), cleaned and sliced
Garlic	3 cloves, peeled and chopped
Salt and pepper	to taste
Parsley	1 sprig, finely chopped

METHOD

• Heat oil in a pan until hot and add mushrooms. Cook until slightly browned.

• Add garlic, salt and pepper. Drain off excess water.

• Place in serving bowls and sprinkle parsley on top.

Photograph on page 28

Front: Eggs Over Easy with Tomatoes
Back: Sautéed Garlic Mushrooms

eggs over easy with tomatoes Serves 2

INGREDIENTS

Olive oil	4 Tbsp
Onion	1, peeled and sliced
Tomatoes	500 g (1 lb 1½ oz), seeded and chopped
Tomato paste	2 Tbsp
Salt and pepper	to taste
Paprika	a pinch
Eggs	4
Parsley	1 sprig, chopped
Dill	1 sprig

METHOD

• Heat olive oil in a pan and sauté onion until fragrant.

• Add tomatoes and tomato paste and stir well. Season with salt, pepper and paprika.

• Break eggs one by one into the tomato sauce and continue to cook until the egg whites are firm.

• Place 2 eggs on each serving dish. Sprinkle parsley on top and garnish with dill. Serve immediately.

seafood tagliatelle with sun-dried tomatoes
Serves 2

INGREDIENTS

Tagliatelle	225 g (8 oz)
Olive oil	4 Tbsp
Garlic	2 cloves, sliced
Clams	225 g (8 oz)
Prawns (shrimps)	225 g (8 oz), peeled and deveined
Salt and pepper	to taste
Sun-dried tomatoes	15 g ($\frac{1}{2}$ oz), chopped
Parsley	15 g ($\frac{1}{2}$ oz), chopped
Freshly ground black pepper	2 Tbsp
Oregano	1 sprig

METHOD

- Cook tagliatelle in boiling water for 8–10 minutes until al dente and drain well.

- Heat olive oil in a large frying pan and sauté garlic until soft.

- Add clams and prawns and stir-fry until prawns are pink. Season with salt and pepper and cook for another 3 minutes.

- Add tomatoes and parsley to tagliatelle and toss well. Pour seafood over tagliatelle and season with black pepper. Mix well.

- Dish out and garnish with oregano leaves. Serve hot.

vegetarian paella Serves 2

INGREDIENTS

Olive oil	2 Tbsp
Onion	1, large, peeled and chopped
Chicken stock (page 9)	1.25 litres (40 fl oz / 5 cups)
Calrose rice	300 g (10½ oz)
Red capsicum (bell pepper)	1, chopped
Saffron threads	a pinch
Tomatoes	4, peeled, seeded and chopped
Frozen peas	250 g (9 oz)
Coriander leaves (cilantro)	1 sprig
Broccoli	125 g (4½ oz), cut into bite-size pieces

NOTE

Calrose rice is a medium grain variety of rice. It is used in this recipe as it absorbs flavour well. If unavailable, you can use any short grain rice such as sushi rice or arborio.

METHOD

- Heat oil in pan and stir-fry onion until soft.

- Add chicken stock, rice, capsicum and saffron.

- Add tomatoes and cook until stock is absorbed. Stir until mixture boils and rice is almost tender.

- Add peas and cook covered for about 10 minutes.

- Dish out and garnish with coriander leaves and serve hot.

rosemary crabmeat omelette Serves 2

INGREDIENTS

Olive oil	2 Tbsp
Rosemary	2 sprigs
Eggs	4, seasoned with salt and beaten
Crabmeat	125 g (4½ oz)

METHOD

- Heat I Tbsp oil in a pan over medium heat. Sear I sprig rosemary and set aside. Pour half the egg mixture into pan and swirl it around to coat pan.

- Sprinkle half the crabmeat on top and cook until omelette is firm. Repeat steps until mixture is used up to make another omelette.

- Add fried rosemary and roll omelette up. Place on a plate Garnish as desired and serve hot.

rack of lamb with rosemary potatoes Serves 2

INGREDIENTS

Rack of lamb	1/2, trimmed
Dijon mustard	2 tsp
Salt and pepper	to taste
Olive oil	2 Tbsp
Oregano	1 sprig

POTATOES

Red potatoes	450 g (1 lb), peeled and thinly sliced
Vegetable oil	1 Tbsp
Rosemary	1 sprig
Salt and pepper	to taste

N O T E
Half a rack of lamb can be substituted with 8 ribs.

METHOD

- Preheat oven to 230°C (450°F).

- Season lamb with mustard, salt and pepper.

- Heat 1 Tbsp olive oil in a large ovenproof pan and sear lamb for 1–2 minutes on all sides. Remove from heat and set aside for a few minutes.

- Roast lamb in preheated oven for 5–7 minutes. Remove from oven and let it rest for 3–5 minutes.

- Prepare potatoes. Boil potatoes until half cooked and place in a roasting pan. Toss with oil, rosemary, salt and pepper until evenly coated. Spread potatoes out in a single layer and bake in the oven for 20 minutes.

- Serve lamb with potatoes.

Front: Rack of Lamb with Rosemary Potatoes
Back: French Bean and Tuna Salad

french bean and tuna salad Serves 2

INGREDIENTS

French beans	500 g (1 lb 1 1/2 oz), blanched
Onion	1, peeled and thinly sliced
Cherry tomatoes	50 g (2 oz), quartered
Canned flaked tuna	140 g (5 oz), drained
Salt and pepper	to taste
Extra virgin olive oil	1 Tbsp
White vinegar	1 tsp
Oregano	1 sprig

METHOD

• Combine French beans, onion, tomatoes and tuna flakes in a bowl and mix well. Sprinkle with salt and pepper.

• In a separate bowl, whisk olive oil and vinegar until well combined. Drizzle over salad.

• Garnish with oregano and serve immediately.

Photograph on page 37

cream cheese with raspberry sauce Serves 2

INGREDIENTS

Cream cheese	300 g (10½ oz)
Icing (confectioner's) sugar	50 g (2 oz)
Whipping cream	250 ml (8 fl oz / 1 cup)
Gooseberries	2
Cinnamon powder	1 tsp

SAUCE

Raspberries	200 g (7 oz)
Icing (confectioner's) sugar	30 g (1 oz)
Lemon juice	to taste
Water	150 ml (5 fl oz)

METHOD

• Whisk cream cheese in a bowl, stirring in icing sugar and whipping cream gradually until smooth.

• Spoon cheese mixture in 2 ring moulds and chill in the refrigerator for at least 30 minutes or until set.

• Remove set cream cheese from moulds and place on a serving dish.

• To make sauce, combine all the ingredients in a food processor and blend until smooth. Strain well.

• To serve, drizzle sauce over cream cheese. Garnish with gooseberries and sprinkle cinnamon powder over. Serve cold.

Photograph on page 40

Front: Penne Rigate with Basil and Garlic Butter
Back: Cream Cheese with Raspberry Sauce

penne rigate with basil and garlic butter Serves 2

INGREDIENTS

Penne rigate	300 g (10½ oz)
Butter	85 g (3 oz)
Olive oil	3 Tbsp
Garlic	4 cloves, peeled and finely chopped
Basil	1 bunch, finely shredded + more for garnishing
Salt and pepper	to taste

METHOD

- Bring a pot of water and cook penne according to packet instructions. Drain and set aside.

- Heat butter and olive oil in a pan over medium heat and fry garlic until fragrant.

- Add basil and increase heat. Be careful not to burn basil.

- Toss pasta in the mixture and season with salt and pepper.

- Dish out and garnish with some basil. Serve hot.

beef goulash Serves 2

INGREDIENTS

Beef	250 g (9 oz), cubed
Salt and pepper	to taste
Olive oil	1 tsp
Onion	1, peeled and chopped
Garlic	3 cloves, peeled and crushed
Basil	2 leaves
Oregano	1 tsp
Tomato paste	2 tsp
Tomatoes	3, diced
Water	2 litres (64 fl oz / 8 cups)
Potatoes	2, large, peeled and diced
Carrot	1, peeled and diced
Chevril	1 sprig

METHOD

• Season beef with salt and pepper.

• Heat oil in a large frying pan and sear beef until golden brown. Remove from heat and set aside.

• Sauté onion, garlic, basil and oregano until fragrant.

• Stir in tomato paste and add tomatoes. Add water while continually stirring.

• Return beef to the pan and add potatoes and carrot. Cook until tender. Season to taste.

• Dish out and garnish with chevril. Serve immediately.

pepper rice Serves 2

INGREDIENTS

Butter	45 g (1½ oz)
Long-grain rice	125 g (4½ oz)
Water	375 ml (12 fl oz / 1½ cups)
Green, yellow and red capsicums (bell peppers)	1 each, seeded and diced
Salt	to taste
Freshly ground black pepper	1 tsp
Parsley	1 sprig

METHOD

- Melt butter in a large pan over medium heat.

- Add rice and stir until rice is translucent but not browned. Add water and mix well. Bring mixture to a boil.

- Cover pan and reduce heat to low. Simmer until rice is cooked. Add capsicums in the last 10 minutes of cooking.

- Season with salt and dish out onto serving plates.

- Sprinkle black pepper over rice and top with parsley. Serve hot.

tarragon-infused sea bass Serves 2

INGREDIENTS

Sea bass fillets	4, about 175 g (6 oz) each
Tarragon	30 g (1 oz)
Extra virgin olive oil	1 tsp
Lemon juice	from 1 lemon
Salt and pepper	to taste
Basil	1 sprig
Dill	1 sprig
Alfalfa sprouts	1 Tbsp

METHOD

- Heat grill or pan. Coat fish fillets with one-quarter of tarragon leaves and cook for 3 minutes.

- Turn fish over and continue cooking fish for another 3 minutes.

- Drizzle olive oil and lemon juice over fish. Season with salt and pepper.

- Arrange basil leaves on serving plates and place fish on top. Garnish with dill and alfalfa sprouts. Serve hot.

baked veal with apples and tarragon Serves 2

INGREDIENTS

Sunflower oil	2 Tbsp
Veal chops	4 pieces, trimmed
Onion	1, peeled and finely sliced
Dessert apples	2, cored and sliced
Sultanas	30 g (1 oz)
Unsweetened apple juice	125 ml (4 fl oz / ½ cup)
Salt and pepper	to taste
Chevril	1 sprig
Red capsicum (bell pepper)	½, thinly sliced

METHOD

- Heat oil in a casserole dish and fry veal chops for 3–4 minutes or until lightly browned.

- Add onion and apples and fry for a further 2 minutes.

- Stir in sultanas and apple juice. Season with salt and pepper.

- Cover casserole dish and place in a preheated oven at 190°C (375°F). Bake for 50 minutes or until veal is tender.

- Arrange veal on serving plates and pour gravy over. Garnish with chevril and red capsicum. Serve hot.

linguine in clam sauce Serves 2

INGREDIENTS

Linguine	300 g (10½ oz)
Olive oil	4 Tbsp
Grated ginger	1 Tbsp
Garlic	4 cloves, peeled and finely chopped
Fermented black beans	1 Tbsp, soaked, drained and chopped
Sugar	to taste
Light soy sauce	2 Tbsp
Clams	500 g (1 lb 1½ oz), scrubbed and cleaned
Sesame oil	2 tsp
Bird's eye chillies	4, finely sliced
Sage	1 sprig

METHOD

• Bring a pot of water and cook linguine according to packet instructions. Drain and set aside.

• Heat olive oil in a pan and sauté ginger, garlic and black beans for 1 minute.

• Add sugar, soy sauce and clams. Cover and cook over high heat until clams are cooked. Discard any clams that are unopened.

• Add sesame oil and linguine and toss well.

• Dish out and garnish with bird's eye chillies and sage. Serve hot.

grilled tiger prawns with vegetable medley
Serves 2

INGREDIENTS

Tiger prawns (shrimps)	200 g (7 oz), sliced and deveined
Salt and pepper	to taste
Thai sweet chilli sauce	3 Tbsp
Alfalfa sprouts	1 Tbsp
Chinese chives	1 sprig

VEGETABLE MEDLEY

Olive oil	1 tsp
Red capsicum (bell pepper)	1, sliced into 1-cm (1/2-in) strips
Garlic pepper	1 tsp
Yellow squash	1, sliced into 1-cm (1/2-in) strips
Courgette (zucchini)	1, sliced into 1-cm (1/2-in) strips
Cayenne pepper	1 tsp
Salt and pepper	to taste

METHOD

- Season prawns with salt and pepper. Set aside for 5 minutes.

- Grill prawns in a pan. Remove when cooked and set aside.

- Prepare vegetable medley. Heat olive oil in a pan and add capsicum. Cook over medium heat for 5 minutes. Add garlic pepper.

- Stir in squash and courgette. Season with cayenne pepper, salt and pepper.

- Remove vegetables from pan and arrange on serving dishes.

- Arrange prawns on top of vegetables and garnish with alfalfa sprouts and Chinese chives. Serve hot.

grilled chicken breast with
honey mustard dressing Serves 2

INGREDIENTS

Chicken breast	1, deboned
Salt and pepper	to taste
Cos lettuce	100 g (3$^1/_2$-in)
Alfalfa sprouts	1 Tbsp

DRESSING

Mayonnaise	4 Tbsp
Mustard	1 Tbsp
Honey	1 Tbsp
Lemon juice	$^1/_2$ Tbsp

METHOD

• Whisk ingredients for dressing in a bowl and leave to cool in the refrigerator.

• Season chicken breast and grill on a frying pan for 10 minutes or until cooked through. Remove from pan and slice thinly.

• Arrange cos lettuce on serving dishes and place chicken on top. Garnish with alfalfa sprouts.

• Drizzle dressing on top of chicken and serve hot.

honeyed apples with dates and nuts Makes 4

INGREDIENTS

Red cooking apples	4, medium, cored
Orange juice	4 Tbsp
Chopped mixed nuts	1 Tbsp, toasted
Chopped dried dates	1 Tbsp
Lemon juice	from $\frac{1}{2}$ lemon
Ground cinnamon	$\frac{1}{2}$ tsp
Canned raspberries	3, syrup reserved
Honey	2 Tbsp
Bay leaf	1

METHOD

• Wash apples and peel the upper half.

• Heat orange juice in a pan and glaze apples in the orange juice. Remove from heat after 1 minute and place apples in an ovenproof dish.

• Mix the remaining ingredients, except honey and bay leaf, in a bowl and stuff apples with mixture.

• Drizzle honey over the apples, cover with aluminium foil and place on a baking dish. Bake in a preheated oven at 190°C (375°F).

• Remove foil and place on a serving dish. Arrange raspberries on serving dish and top apple with bay leaf. Serve warm.

pistachio-chocolate and cinnamon homemade ice cream Serves 2

INGREDIENTS

Milk	500 ml (16 fl oz / 2 cups)
Cinnamon	2 sticks, halved
Bittersweet chocolate	170 g (6 oz), finely chopped
Egg yolks	8
Castor sugar	110 g (4 oz)
Double (heavy) cream	300 ml (10 fl oz / 1 1/4 cups)
Pistachio nuts	125 g (4 1/2 oz), chopped

METHOD

- Place milk, cinnamon and chocolate in a large pan. Stir over low heat until chocolate is melted.

- Remove mixture from heat and let it stand for 5 minutes. Strain into a jug and discard cinnamon sticks.

- Beat egg yolks and sugar in a small bowl with an electric mixer until thick. Gradually add hot chocolate mixture until well mixed.

- Return mixture to the pan and stir over low heat, without boiling for about 15 minutes or until mixture thickens.

- Remove from heat and transfer mixture into a large bowl. Cover and refrigerate for 1 hour or until cold.

- Stir in cream, then pour mixture into a pan and cover with aluminium foil. Freeze for several hours or until firm.

- Beat frozen mixture with an electric mixer until smooth. Return mixture to the same pan and cover with aluminium foil. Continue to freeze until firm.

- Serve ice cream with pistachios. Garnish as desired.

poached pear with chocolate sauce Serves 2

INGREDIENTS

Sparkling white wine	750 ml (24 fl oz / 3 cups)
Orange juice	125 ml (4 fl oz / $^1/_2$ cup)
Castor sugar	100 g ($3^1/_2$ oz)
Orange	2 slices
Ground cloves	2 tsp
Cinnamon	1 stick, about 2-cm (1-in) long
Chinese pears	2, peeled, leaving stems intact
Semi-sweet chocolate chips	55 g (2 oz)
Mint	1 sprig

METHOD

- Combine sparkling wine, orange juice and sugar in a saucepan over medium heat.

- Add orange, cloves and cinnamon. Bring mixture to the boil and stir until sugar is dissolved.

- Place Chinese pears in the saucepan and reduce heat. Cover and simmer for 15 minutes.

- Remove lid and simmer for another 30 minutes. Remove pears from heat and set aside to cool.

- Melt chocolate chips in a bain-marie, stirring until melted.

- Drizzle pears with melted chocolate and garnish with mint. Serve immediately.

chocolate baba with basil orange yoghurt

Serves 2

INGREDIENTS

Butter	55 g (2 oz)
Cocoa powder	2 Tbsp
Dark chocolate	70 g (2^1/$_2$ oz), chopped
Egg yolks	2
Icing (confectioner's) sugar	60 g (2 oz) + more for dusting
Plain (all-purpose) flour	40 g (1^1/$_4$ oz)
Baking powder	1 tsp
Mint	1 sprig
Orange zest	from ^{1}/$_2$ orange, thinly sliced

BASIL ORANGE YOGHURT

Plain yoghurt	500 ml (16 fl oz / 2 cups)
Castor sugar	30 g (1 oz)
Basil	a few sprigs, finely shredded
Orange	^{1}/$_2$, peeled and finely diced

METHOD

• Preheat oven to 180°C (350°F).

• Lightly grease and powder ramekins with butter and cocoa powder. Place in the refrigerator.

• Melt 1 tsp butter and chocolate in a bain-marie, stirring gently.

• Mix egg yolks in a bowl and add icing sugar, flour, baking powder and 1 tsp cocoa powder. Gently fold in melted chocolate. Fill ramekins and bake for 7 minutes.

• Prepare basil orange yoghurt. Combine all the ingredients, except orange, in a food processor and blend well. Add orange and mix well.

• Garnish chocolate pudding with mint and orange zest. Dust with a little icing sugar and serve with basil orange yoghurt.

crème fraiche with fruit Serves 2

INGREDIENTS

Canned peaches	1/2, drained and diced
Canned pears	1/2, drained and diced
Canned pineapples	10 chunks, chopped
Mint	1 sprig
Cocoa powder	2 Tbsp

CRÈME FRAICHE

Double (heavy) cream	300 ml (10 fl oz / 1 1/4 cups)
Sour cream	300 ml (10 fl oz / 1 1/4 cups)
Castor sugar	1 Tbsp

METHOD

- Start preparations 1–2 days ahead. Prepare crème fraiche. Combine cream and sour cream in a bowl and cover. Leave to stand for 1–2 days until mixture is thickened.

- Stir in sugar, cover and refrigerate to chill before using.

- Spoon some fruit into 2 serving cups or bowls and top with crème fraiche. Repeat to layer with more fruit and crème fraiche.

- Garnish with mint and dust cocoa powder over. Serve cold.

coconut crème brûlée Serves 2

INGREDIENTS

Coconut milk	500 ml (16 fl oz / 2 cups)
Egg yolks	8
Castor sugar	100 g (3½ oz) + more for caramelising crème brûlée
Grated coconut	3 Tbsp, finely ground
Cocoa powder	1 Tbsp
Mint	1 sprig

METHOD

- Heat coconut milk in a small pan.

- Meanwhile, combine egg yolks and sugar in a bowl and whisk until sugar dissolves.

- Add warm coconut milk to mixture and stir well to combine.

- Divide mixture equally between 2 individual ramekins and arrange ramekins in a *bain-marie*. Bake in a preheated oven at 150°C (300°F) for 30–40 minutes.

- Place grated coconut in a small pan and fry on low heat until golden brown. Remove from heat and set aside.

- Remove crème brûlée from oven and leave to cool. Sprinkle sugar over cooled crème brûlée and return to the oven. Grill until sugar caramelises.

- Remove from oven and unmould crème brûlée, if desired. Top crème brûlée with grated coconut. Dust with some cocoa powder and garnish with mint leaves. Serve warm.

mango-passion fruit crumble Serves 2

INGREDIENTS

Ripe mangoes	2, peeled and diced
Passion fruit	2, peeled and diced
Sour cream	375 ml (12 fl oz / 1 1/2 cups)
Castor sugar	1 Tbsp
Egg	1
Plain (all-purpose) flour	1 Tbsp
Orange zest	1 tsp
Sugared preserved sour plums	3, sliced
Gooseberries	2

CRUMBLE

Plain (all-purpose) flour	170 g (6 oz)
Brown sugar	85 g (3 oz)
Lemon zest	from 1/2 lemon
Cinnamon powder	1/2 tsp
Butter	90 g (3 oz), cut into cubes

METHOD

• Preheat oven to 180°C (350°F).

• Combine mangoes and passion fruit in an ovenproof dish.

• Combine sour cream, sugar, egg and flour in a bowl and beat until smooth. Pour mixture over fruit.

• Make crumble. Combine flour, sugar, lemon zest and cinnamon, then rub in butter until mixture resembles bread crumbs. Sprinkle crumble over fruit mixture.

• Bake for 30 minutes or until golden brown. Remove from oven and set aside to cool slightly.

• Spoon crumble into serving bowls and garnish with orange zest, sugared preserved sour plums and gooseberries. Serve warm.

red bean crêpes with orange sauce Serves 2

INGREDIENTS

Cooking oil	as needed
Red bean paste	8 Tbsp
Butter	2 Tbsp
Mint	1 sprig

CRÊPE BATTER

Plain (all-purpose) flour	15 g ($^1/_2$ oz)
Salt	1 tsp
Eggs	3
Water	250 ml (8 fl oz / 1 cup)
Butter	2 Tbsp, softened
Milk	250 ml (8 fl oz / 1 cup)

ORANGE SAUCE

Castor sugar	70 g ($2^1/_2$ oz)
Butter	45 g ($1^1/_2$ oz)
Orange juice	3 Tbsp
Orange	$^1/_4$, segmented

METHOD

- Prepare crêpe batter. Sift flour and salt into a bowl and make a well in the centre.

- Crack eggs into the well and beat well. When mixture starts to thicken, add water, butter and half the milk.

- Beat mixture until smooth, then add remaining milk. Strain through a fine-mesh sieve to remove any lumps. Store in a covered container in the refrigerator while preparing other ingredients.

- To make orange sauce, combine all ingredients in a saucepan and heat over medium heat. Stir well and bring to a boil.

- Reduce heat and simmer for another 5 minutes. Remove from heat and set aside.

- Heat a pan and coat it with oil Pour in a ladle of chilled batter and swirl batter around to make a thin crêpes. Cook over low heat until golden brown. Repeat this until batter is used up.

- Place 2 Tbsp red bean paste on each crêpe and roll up with the ends folded in. Dot with butter and lightly fry on a pan.

- Place crêpes on a serving dish, drizzle orange sauce over, garnish with mint. Serve warm.

weights and measures

Quantities for this book are given in Metric, Imperial and American (spoon and cup) measures. Standard spoon and cup measurements used are: 1 tsp = 5 ml, 1 Tbsp = 15 ml, 1 cup = 250 ml. All measures are level unless otherwise stated.

Liquid And Volume Measures

Metric	Imperial	American
5 ml	1/6 fl oz	1 teaspoon
10 ml	1/3 fl oz	1 dessertspoon
15 ml	1/2 fl oz	1 tablespoon
60 ml	2 fl oz	1/4 cup (4 tablespoons)
85 ml	2 1/2 fl oz	1/3 cup
90 ml	3 fl oz	3/8 cup (6 tablespoons)
125 ml	4 fl oz	1/2 cup
180 ml	6 fl oz	3/4 cup
250 ml	8 fl oz	1 cup
300 ml	10 fl oz (1/2 pint)	1 1/4 cups
375 ml	12 fl oz	1 1/2 cups
435 ml	14 fl oz	1 3/4 cups
500 ml	16 fl oz	2 cups
625 ml	20 fl oz (1 pint)	2 1/2 cups
750 ml	24 fl oz (1 1/5 pints)	3 cups
1 litre	32 fl oz (1 3/5 pints)	4 cups
1.25 litres	40 fl oz (2 pints)	5 cups
1.5 litres	48 fl oz (2 2/5 pints)	6 cups
2.5 litres	80 fl oz (4 pints)	10 cups

Dry Measures

Metric	Imperial
30 grams	1 ounce
45 grams	1 1/2 ounces
55 grams	2 ounces
70 grams	2 1/2 ounces
85 grams	3 ounces
100 grams	3 1/2 ounces
110 grams	4 ounces
125 grams	4 1/2 ounces
140 grams	5 ounces
280 grams	10 ounces
450 grams	16 ounces (1 pound)
500 grams	1 pound, 1 1/2 ounces
700 grams	1 1/2 pounds
800 grams	1 3/4 pounds
1 kilogram	2 pounds, 3 ounces
1.5 kilograms	3 pounds, 4 1/2 ounces
2 kilograms	4 pounds, 6 ounces

Oven Temperature

	°C	°F	Gas Regulo
Very slow	120	250	1
Slow	150	300	2
Moderately slow	160	325	3
Moderate	180	350	4
Moderately hot	190/200	375/400	5/6
Hot	210/220	410/425	6/7
Very hot	230	450	8
Super hot	250/290	475/550	9/10

Length

Metric	Imperial
0.5 cm	1/4 inch
1 cm	1/2 inch
1.5 cm	3/4 inch
2.5 cm	1 inch

Abbreviation

tsp	teaspoon
Tbsp	tablespoon
g	gram
kg	kilogram
ml	millilitre